The Magical Garden of Sharing

The Wonder of Sharing

James Avino

Copyright © 2025 by James Avino

All Rights Reserved.

This book is subject to the condition that no part of this book is to be reproduced, transmitted in any form or means; electronic or mechanical, stored in a retrieval system, photocopied, recorded, scanned, or otherwise. Any of these actions requires the proper written permission of the author.

To my beautiful granddaughters, Bella, Adri, and Stasi, who fill my heart with endless joy and inspire me every day. You are the magic behind this story, and your kindness, curiosity, and love for one another are the true wonders of the world. May this tale remind you always of the power of sharing and the beauty of growing together.

With all my love,
Poppy

Once upon a time, in a quaint little village, there lived three best friends named Annabella, Adriana, and Anastasia. They were inseparable, and their laughter could often be heard echoing through the village square.

Their houses were side by side, nestled along a cobbled path lined with wildflowers. Every day after their chores, they would run out to play in the village, inventing games, exploring new places, and creating memories together.

One sunny afternoon, the girls decided to wander farther than usual. They were following a butterfly that fluttered through a narrow, winding trail at the edge of the village. The path led them to a hidden corner where a tall, colorful wall of flowers grew wild and thick.

As they brushed the flowers aside, a warm breeze drifted out from behind them, carrying a scent sweeter than anything they had ever smelled. With wide eyes, they stepped through the flowers and found themselves in a mysterious, enchanted garden.

The garden was like something out of a fairy tale. Flowers of every color and shape surrounded them, each one more beautiful than the last. Twinkling lights floated above them, and the trees whispered in gentle voices that seemed to sing about friendship, kindness, and joy.

At the center of the garden stood a peculiar tree, much larger than any they had ever seen. Its branches were heavy with shimmering, magical fruits that glowed softly, as if filled with stardust. The fruits were unlike apples or oranges; they were round, with a hue of cranberry and filled the air with an enchanting scent.

As the girls stepped closer, the tree spoke in a kind and gentle voice,
"Welcome, little ones. You have found the Magical Garden of Sharing.
Here, the magic grows with every act of kindness. And the more you
share, the stronger the magic becomes."

The girls were thrilled. They had never seen a talking tree before! Eager to know more, they reached out to pick one of the magical fruits. The tree whispered their name, "Shareberries."

The moment each girl plucked a Shareberry from the branches, the whole garden began to glow. The flowers opened wider,
the trees swayed in rhythm, and the lights above them sparkled even brighter.

Curious, the girls decided to test the tree's words. Annabella offered her Shareberry to Adriana, who took a small bite and handed it back to her friend. Adriana shared her Shareberry with Anastasia, and Anastasia gave a piece of hers to Annabella. As they each took turns sharing their fruits, an amazing thing happened: the colors around them burst into a radiant symphony, and a magical melody filled the air.

The friends laughed with delight as they felt a warm, joyful energy wrapping around them.

"Wow!" Annabella exclaimed. "It really does work! Look how happy the garden is!"

The tree, pleased with their joy, spoke again,
"In the Magical Garden of Sharing, every act of kindness creates magic.
The more you share, the more beautiful the world becomes."

Overwhelmed with excitement, the friends decided to keep sharing, not only their Shareberries but everything they had. Annabella offered her hair ribbon to Adriana, who tied it around her wrist as a friendship bracelet. Adriana shared her little bag of marbles with Anastasia, who taught the others a new game. Anastasia then shared her favorite storybook with Annabella, and they sat together, giggling over the tales.

With each new act of sharing, the garden grew more vibrant. Butterflies appeared in swarms, flowers danced in waves of color, and birds began to sing cheerful tunes from the branches above. The magic of the garden filled them with a happiness they had never felt before.

Word of the magical garden soon spread throughout the village, and other children were drawn to the laughter and joy echoing from within. One by one, they joined Annabella, Adriana, and Anastasia in the garden, each bringing something to share. Some brought toys, others brought snacks, and some even brought stories of their own.

Days passed, and the garden transformed. One morning, the children noticed that the Shareberries had blossomed into delicate, colorful flowers. The tree explained that these were "Friendship Flowers," a gift from the garden to everyone who had shared and spread kindness. The flowers symbolized the strong bonds they had created together, blooming in every color imaginable, each petal a reminder of the joy that comes from giving.

The garden quickly became the heart of the village, a place where everyone gathered to play, share, and enjoy each other's company. Even the grown-ups joined in, charmed by the children's tales of the garden's magic. Neighbors who rarely spoke to each other before began sharing their favorite recipes, telling stories from their own childhoods, and laughing together over shared memories. The once-divided village grew closer, bound by the magic of friendship and kindness.

Over time, the children learned that the garden's magic didn't stay confined within its walls. They found that whenever they shared outside the garden—whether it was offering a helping hand, sharing a kind word, or lending a toy—the same warm feeling would surround them. The garden had taught them that the true magic of sharing could exist anywhere, as long as it came from the heart.

And so, Annabella, Adriana, and Anastasia continued to visit the Magical Garden of Sharing, sometimes with friends and sometimes just the three of them. They never forgot the lessons they learned there, and every visit reminded them that sharing was not only rewarding but also the key to a world filled with happiness and friendship.

The garden's magic never faded, for each new generation of children discovered its wonders, spreading its message of kindness, generosity, and joy throughout the village and beyond. And they all lived happily ever after, their hearts forever touched by the magic of sharing.

www.ingramcontent.com/pod-product-compliance
Lightning Source LLC
Chambersburg PA
CBHW041121070526
44584CB00002B/230